7 WAYS TO PAY MORE FOR YOUR MORTGAGE

or not

PLANNING STEPS THAT CAN SAVE YOU A BUNDLE!

TRACIA LARIMER

Disclaimer

The author and publisher assume no responsibility or liability for any errors or omissions in the content of this book. Although we believe the facts presented are accurate as of the date it was written.

The information provided in this book is designed to provide helpful information on the subjects discussed. The views and opinions expressed in this book are those of the authors and do not necessarily reflect the views of other mortgage brokers or lenders. Also, laws and practices sometimes vary between states and are subject to change.

All client examples are a composite character based on many individuals I have worked with throughout the years. Any resemblance to actual persons, living or dead, or actual events is purely coincidental.

The author and publisher specifically disclaim any liability resulting from the use or application of information contained in this book, and the information is not intended to serve as legal, financial or other professional advice related to individual situations.

Printed in the United States of America
First Printing, November 5th 2018
ISBN 978-0-692-18082-2
Azara Capital Solutions, LLC
Bend, Oregon

Table of Contents

Introduction

Want to pay extra for your mortgage?

Of course not.

No one wants to pay more for their mortgage than they have to, but everyday pitfalls caused by money mistakes can result in exactly that.

So let's figure out how to sidestep them so you can get the most affordable mortgage possible.

AVOIDING PITFALLS CAN AVOID HIGHER INTEREST COSTS

It all starts with how your interest rate is determined. The lender will offer you a rate that investors on the secondary market are willing to buy. This rate is determined by your credit score, home location, home price, loan amount and how much you're able to put towards a down payment.

Other factors that determine rates are the loan term and the type of mortgage you're seeking, and whether you're refinancing a current mortgage for more than you owe and are taking the difference in cash.

Property type also comes into play. For instance, is the home manufactured or stick-built? Is it a single-family residence or a multiplex? Are you occupying the property or are you purchasing it as an investment?

Lender credits and points, allow you to make choices about your interest rate. You can opt for a zero-point loan, or a lender credit which is used to pay some or all of your closing costs in exchange for a slightly higher rate. Either of these options can be worthwhile if you know this home isn't your forever home or you expect that you'll refinance the mortgage down the road.

Closing costs are fees that are associated with getting a mortgage. The types of fees you can expect include but are not limited to: appraisal and credit report fees, escrow and title fees, lender fees and recording fees. Having a lender credit can offset these fees which are in addition to your down payment.

If you plan to live in the home for a long time and don't foresee selling your home or refinancing the current mortgage in the near future, then forgoing the lender credit and opting to pay discount points can also be an option. Discount points are in exchange for a lower interest rate and the amount that you'll pay varies depending on the interest rate you choose.

It's worthwhile having your lender calculate how long it will take you to recoup the cost of the discount points verses paying zero points or receiving a lender credit. If you have decided you want the lowest interest rate possible, consider how many years it will take after paying the discount points to recover the cost of this upfront fee. Ask yourself if this is the best use of these funds?

The everyday pitfalls that follow can impact your credit, income and assets and will cause you to pay more for your mortgage. Any increase in your rate, whether it's a slight increase or quite a bit over a conventional rate, may not only cost you a bundle over the life of the loan but can also potentially prevent you from qualifying for the mortgage you want. And who wants that? Knowing these pitfalls in advance can help you not only plan better but reduce financial stress when you put these ideas into action.

Pitfall #1:

SHARING A CREDIT CARD ACCOUNT CAN BE COSTLY

"You're cute and all but I'm not sharing my coffee."

–Author unknown

Did you know that sharing a credit card as a joint card holder can cost you dearly down the road?

When you fall in love, get married or move in together, you expect that this wonderful beginning will last the rest of your life. You're so sure this person is your forever person that you decide to share money and apply for joint credit cards. Of course, it makes sense to have everything in one pot as you merge your lives together.

While this works well for those people who really have met their forever person, for others it can be disastrous.

No one ever wants to plan for the possibility of a breakup. That's like entering the relationship with a half commitment and an escape plan. I even debated if I should include this chapter since it seems so negative. Over many years working with clients and helping them get mortgages, however, I have seen firsthand the negative financial consequences of shared credit cards after a breakup.

When you have a shared credit card you are both responsible for any outstanding debt that has been charged. This means that the debt is reported on both your credit reports. This has the potential to become costly to you if the relationship goes south and the credit card debt has been awarded to your ex-spouse.

I know. This seems counterintuitive since that person is now solely responsible for paying off the debt. But an ex-spouse or partner who is awarded this joint credit card debt may not always be able to make the required payments. If payments are late or the debt goes into default, this information will also be reported on *your* credit report, robbing you of your well-earned good credit score. Plus, if the credit card has a balance due that exceeds 30 percent of the available credit or is maxed out, that will also lower your score. A lower score may increase your mortgage interest rate if you decide to purchase a home or refinance an existing mortgage. Once the debt is current and the balance is paid down you will see a score improvement over time.

It doesn't seem fair when an ex-spouse has been awarded the debt but creditors continue to hold you responsible. Unfortunately, this is because when you are a joint account holder, the bank will continue to hold you responsible and continue to report the debt on your credit report as long as the debt exists and long after the partnership or marriage is over. Since the bank is not a party to your divorce, they won't recognize the divorce decree that states the debt was awarded to your spouse.

A WORD ABOUT CREDIT SCORING

To fully understand the impact of this, it's important to understand the credit scoring system. Your credit score is an important asset when buying a home or refinancing a current loan. It's an asset that can allow you to move forward with your life because it will make obtaining credit easier. It's a three-digit statistical number that is provided by each of the credit bureaus. This system evaluates your creditworthiness and is based on your credit history. Lenders use these scores as a risk management tool to evaluate the probability that you'll repay your debts.

When you apply for a mortgage, your interest rate and how much the lender is willing to loan to you is based in part on your credit worthiness. The lender uses the middle score that has been reported by the three main bureaus, Equifax, Experian and Transunion to qualify you. While your credit score is important, other factors such as income, assets and financial stability are also considered when it comes to approving your mortgage loan request.

CONSIDER BECOMING AN AUTHORIZED USER

If you still prefer to share a credit card even after knowing all this, then why not consider adding yourself as an authorized user? As an authorized user you'll receive a card with your name on it and you can be easily taken off down the road if necessary. Conversely, if you're the one with the credit card, you can easily revoke your partner's authorized user privileges. Adding an authorized user is not only a better option if you're part of a couple, you can also add a child to help them build credit. While any expenses that are charged on the card are the ultimate responsibility of the primary account holder, many credit card companies and banks will report on the authorized user's credit up until the time they are taken off the account. Check the policies for your credit card company.

On the other hand, if you've opted to share the card as a joint account holder and you no longer want to be responsible for this debt, your only option will be to close the account. Sounds like a clean and easy solution, right? Not really. If there's a balance owing, even though you will have prevented future debt from being charged, closing the card may hurt your credit scores. Your credit scores will drop because you'll lose the available credit on the card while retaining the debt which impacts your credit utilization ratio (how much you owe versus your credit limit).

Either way, establishing credit in your own name is important for all kinds of reasons even if you are about to be added to a credit card as an authorized user. Having your own credit will help you build your own credit rating, which may come in useful when life tosses unexpected chaos your way.

BUILD A CREDIT HISTORY INDEPENDENTLY

If you choose not to become an authorized user (or don't have that option) and you need to rebuild credit or begin developing a credit history that represents how reliable you are in making your monthly debt payments, obtaining a secured credit card is a good place to start. A secured credit card requires a cash deposit that becomes a credit line for your account. Consider starting with only a $200 or $300 deposit since the bank will hold your money as collateral without paying you interest. This deposit is typically refunded once you close out the card.

Charge no more than 30 percent of the available balance and either pay it off each month or make payments. If you opt to make payments on the card, you'll also be paying interest on the average daily balance. Yes, these companies are cheeky with their expectations and it's an all-around win-win for them.

Putting this aside, a secured credit card is a great way to get your foot in the door and establish your own credit rating. Use the card for six months then apply for an unsecured credit card. If your payment history has been excellent with the secured card, then most likely you'll have no difficulty getting approved for the unsecured one. A word to the wise, only apply for a card that you are likely to get rather than the one that you necessarily want. The best credit cards generally go to people who have high credit scores and an established credit history. When you're starting to build a credit profile, research which cards are recommended for your situation. Companies such as Credit Karma (www. creditkarma.com) can assist with this.

I recommend that you only apply to one bank at a time since each time you apply the inquiry will show up on your credit report costing you points on your score. Also, a number of inquiries in a short period of time may give a bank a reason to reject your application since they will be privy to all banks who are inquiring into your credit. Since multiple inquires in a short time frame are a red flag to a lender, take the time to be strategic when you apply. Multiple inquires make you look like you are desperate, and desperate customers are risky for business.

ACTION ITEM

1. If you need to establish your own credit, I recommend Open Sky (www.openskycc.com). I like this company because, for starters, they don't pull a credit report and create a credit inquiry when you apply. Another benefit is that they begin reporting to the three major bureaus at the end of the first billing cycle. This quick reporting allows you to begin building a credit profile immediately.

2. If you currently have a shared credit card, check company policies regarding any account holder changes. It's a good idea to know these policies in advance so that if a situation should ever arise where you no longer wish to share this debt, you'll be able to implement a strategic plan moving forward.

Pitfall #2:

INSUFFICIENT SAVINGS WILL COST YOU

*"Ask yourself if what you're doing today will
get you closer to where you want to be tomorrow."*

–Author unknown

Nest egg savings can help you save on your next mortgage in a number of ways. If you are buying a new home, a savings account may give you the option for a larger down payment. Higher down payments will often qualify you for a better interest rate. If you are purchasing a home with a small down payment then mortgage insurance may be required and this is an additional cost to home ownership.

Another benefit to having access to nest egg savings is that you'll most likely decrease your reliance on credit cards, thus improving your credit scores. If you recall I discussed this in the first chapter. Higher credit scores can mean a better interest rate when it comes to getting a mortgage as well as other types of financing.

Having additional money left in savings after your loan "funds" (or closes?) is called cash reserves. In certain situations, a lender may require that a borrower has additional financial reserves after their down-payment and closing costs have been paid and they'll ask for proof before your loan "funds" (or closes?).

Having financial reserves after your loan "funds" (or closes?) can also be considered a compensating factor that can override other issues that might prevent you obtaining a full loan approval. When you apply for a mortgage, the lender doesn't only take into account your ability to repay the mortgage, they also look at your overall financial health and liquidity. In other words, the lender's risk is minimized when they know that if a financial emergency occurs you will be able to weather the storm and continue making your monthly mortgage payments.

If cash reserves are required they will consider cash and other assets that are easily converted into cash. Other assets such as your current account balances in savings and checking accounts, funds that came from the selling of an asset, investments in stocks, bonds, mutual funds, money market funds, amount vested in retirement accounts as well as the cash value of a vested life insurance policy. If you are refinancing your current home loan and tapping into some of your equity as a cash-out payment, then this might not be considered part of your cash reserves depending on the lender and type of mortgage.

The minimum amount of reserves required varies depending on whether it's a mortgage for a purchase or a refinance, the occupancy status of the property you are buying or refinancing, whether the property is a single-family residence or has multiple units (such as a duplex or a triplex) or if you own other financed properties.

BENEFITS OF GOING ABOVE AND BEYOND

Bottom line, whether or not you are planning for a mortgage, you know that having a little something stashed away for a rainy day is not only a good idea but can give you more options in life as well as decreasing financial stress and improving credit. With accessible savings you are less reliant on credit cards, and therefore less likely to overuse them.

But why is it so hard to put away those rainy day savings?

My sense is that our culture has moved away from the necessity of savings as credit has become more accessible.

I've often heard over the years statements such as *"I feel secure, I have a lot of available credit if something should happen"* or *"I can always refinance my home and pull out some of my equity"* rather than anticipating using savings for the unexpected. Unfortunately, many discovered that the strategy of continually refinancing a home mortgage to consolidate debt didn't work out as well during the recession years when banks closed open lines of credit and home values plummeted.

There has never been a better time to develop a savings habit in lieu of a steady reliance on credit. If you begin a savings habit today, you'll reap the benefits that come from having more than you need that much sooner. These benefits include fewer sleepless nights worrying about money and less reliance on credit cards. Having savings available to cover any additional costs when you need to dip into an emergency fund will also increase your financial confidence.

A TOUCH OF FINANCIAL PSYCHOLOGY

It may surprise you to hear that achieving a good savings habit seems to have little to do with how much money a person makes. Often the higher a person's income the less savings they have and the more debt they seem to accumulate.

How is this possible you might ask? You may even have noticed that when you know you have additional money coming such as a pay raise, an income tax refund or an inheritance, there's a tendency to start thinking about how you'd like to spend this money before you've received it. Perhaps you even bought some items in advance of receiving the additional income or money. It can also be tempting to charge the purchase on a credit card with the idea that you'll pay it off once the money arrives.

Although not ideal, your home equity can be a financial resource when you most need it. I often help clients who are burdened by debt to consolidate credit cards by using their equity. This type of refinance can put you back in control of your money. You can reduce your monthly debt payments and free up additional cash flow so that you have the additional funds to invest and/or get a fresh start. This approach should not, however, be used as a band-aid for a larger issue such as a spending addiction.

Many years ago, I refinanced a couple's home. They used some of this equity to pay off their credit cards. They shared with me that tapping into their equity/savings was fine since they had an inheritance coming. One problem. They were in a pattern of spending more than they had, but there was no timeline on when this inheritance might arrive. Since this inheritance depended on a family member passing away and they had established a pattern of overspending, it's unlikely that by the time they received the inheritance they would be better off. A pattern of overspending can be a hard one to break and when the money finally arrives my guess is that it will be spent rather than invested. At the end of the day, there's a good chance they could end up not having accumulated any financial assets.

CULTIVATING A NEW HABIT

So how do we get back to establishing a savings habit with less reliance on credit?

A much 'much' younger me with my grandmother

Last summer I spent a lot of time on my porch. The neighborhood squirrels were gathering food to store as the promise of cold winter months loomed ahead. I remembered a conversation I had with my grandmother as a young girl.

I don't recall exactly how old I was when I started earning pocket money for little jobs that had been assigned to me. I do however remember my excitement when payday arrived and how I couldn't wait to go to the store to buy some candy, a book or some other item.

One day my grandmother, observing my anticipation, decided it was time to have "the money conversation". She suggested the importance of saving my pocket money and proposed I make a habit of taking a small portion to reward myself for my efforts while saving the rest. This rainy day savings plan, as she called it, was my first lesson about financial self-care.

A SAVINGS PLAN IS A FOUNDATIONAL STRATEGY

There are many reasons why it's difficult to save in today's world. Although our grandparents lived in a different time with a very different pace to life than we now experience, the wisdom of the past is still relevant today.

Homeownership comes with financial responsibilities that expand beyond saving to purchase a home or making a mortgage payment. There will be times when you'll be grateful for your rainy day savings as you make necessary repairs, pay for general maintenance or even remodel your home as your family needs change.

When it comes to home ownership, a savings plan may be one of your best foundational strategies because it prepares you for the unexpected, rather than having the unexpected propel you into credit card debt and financial plus emotional distress.

ACTION ITEM

If you have already established an excellent savings habit then you might consider meeting with a financial planner to see how you can maximize your savings efforts.

If getting into a savings habit has eluded you in the past, then creating a new habit could be in your best interest. Go easy on yourself as you decide how much you can afford to squirrel away each month. You want this to feel like a win, not a hardship! If the amount you choose to save each month feels like a hardship, you'll sabotage your success fairly quickly. The main point here is to create a new habit you can feel good about.

Start today and make a commitment to saving a percentage of your income. Consider opening a separate account just for your rainy day fund. As I have already mentioned, choose an amount you can stick with each month that's doable for your budget, since with good intentions it's often tempting to overcommit.

If you lack discipline, you could consider limiting your access to your savings by opening your rainy day savings account at a different bank and not carrying the debit card in your wallet.

If you have never really established a savings habit, meet with a financial planner or a money coach. There are many planners who will work with clients who have smaller as well as larger amounts to invest. They can be a fabulous resource in helping you create a workable budget.

Another way to maximize your cashflow so that you are able to save more is to evaluate where your money is being spent. Is it possible that you are overspending unnecessarily in certain areas? For instance, recently I encouraged a client whose insurance cost seemed high to research other companies for a competitive quote. As it turned out, this was *time well spent.* My client 's overall housing expense decreased with the lower insurance cost, plus she saved money on her automobile insurance as well.

Pitfall #3:

CREDIT CARD BALANCES THAT CONTINUE TO INCREASE

"Some debts are fun when you are acquiring them, but none are fun when you set about retiring them."

–Ogden Nash

Credit card balances that continue to increase can lower your credit score. I know we discussed this in the first chapter, but it's worth a reminder. Rule of thumb: anytime you owe more than 30 percent of your overall available credit, your scores will drop proportionately. This rule applies to each individual card as well as the cumulative limit for all your cards. When this occurs, you may find yourself paying a higher interest rate for your next mortgage.

Each time you reach into your wallet and pull out a credit card you might want to think again. That's not as easy as it sounds. Credit card companies have become adept at climbing into our subconscious minds and propelling us towards acceptance and use of their products.

If you are like most of us, you might like to think that your mind belongs to you. However, research has shown how truly vulnerable the human mind is to outside influences. It's this adaptability that allows you to change your life for the better when you make conscious choices and use goal setting as a vehicle to attaining a better life. On the other hand, this vulnerability can instead cause you to make poor choices that you've been persuaded to make from clever sales or advertising strategies. An example of this might be an astute sales person who quickly figures out your unconscious buying triggers and uses this information to sell you a product or service that you might not normally have purchased. It can also be a credit card company's marketing department that through decades of research about human nature has accumulated a well-articulated knowledge database of how their customers make buying decisions. This is how they are able to tune in to your most secret desires and get you to "buy" their card.

You should be furious, but chances are you're not since borrowing money is as old as the hills and as socially acceptable as eating ice cream.

OFFERS FOR CREDIT ARE EVERYWHERE

Today, the world is a much different place than past generations experienced. Your parents, grandparents and ancestors didn't live with the increasing bombardment of advertising that you are now subjected to virtually every minute of every day.

Think about how credit card companies approach you.

While they heavily utilize the Internet along with text, television and radio advertising, they'll also market to you with a more personalized approach. They want you touching and feeling their products and they often achieve this without your consent or agreement.

You may have received letters in the mail with "You're preapproved" stamped in large letters, coupled with a sample card that might even have your name printed on it. As you open the promotion you are greeted with an idea that you can have easy access to money. After all, you are "pre-approved"! Notice that these offers come often enough to ensure that they reach you at your most vulnerable times and also notice how they use visual, kinesthetic (feeling and touching) and emotional verbiage to grab your attention.

Consider the following phrases that have been utilized by credit card companies in their attempts to influence you to accept their products:

"Splash into Cash"
"Countdown to Financial Victory with Extra Cash
– Today's Solutions"
"Live Richly"
"Tomorrow's Dreams"
"Request the Credit That You Deserve Today"

Combine all of this with auditory phrases such as "what's in your wallet?" or "I got my money" and it doesn't take long for them to own your decisions!

What does a simple statement such as "Live Richly" really say to you? You are sold the idea that debt will give you a rich life; that debt will give you a free life; and that debt is adventure. Nowhere in any of these advertisements does it remind you that *"Splashing into Cash"* today can cause financial and emotional stress tomorrow.

As these companies continue to repeatedly parade their offers before your eyes, ears and emotions, it could be easy for you to begin to believe the idea that you, too, can live richly without the necessary resources to have a rich life. This "living richly" concept can take you down a path of over-consumption with fewer savings and more debt, especially if you are in a more vulnerable place in life such as experiencing the loss of a loved one or a large unexpected home repair.

If you are buying your first home or are a returning homeowner, hold on to your hat!

Because as a homeowner, you are now considered an even better credit risk. You will be bombarded with even more credit card offers and these offers will come with higher credit limits.

It's easy for this promise of credit to derail you from a savings plan that will cover the unplanned expenses that come with homeownership.

EXPLORE OPEN SPACE WITH COMFORT

Why do credit card companies work so hard to get you to carry their particular card in your wallet?

Did you know that research has shown that if you are like most people, just having a credit card in your wallet will cause you to pay more for goods and services? I have a personal theory on why this might be so. I think it has to do with the open space that's created with open and unused lines of credit. If you think about this, it's not uncommon to talk about credit cards being maxed out, which to me says there's no more open space.

I believe that that some part of the complex psychology of the brain doesn't know what to do with open space, which instinctively causes us to try to fill this space to avoid subtle discomfort. I wonder if a scientist or doctor might have a fancy phrase for this? Since I lack scientific fortitude, my theory is based only on general observation.

You may have noticed your own need to fill open space when moving from a smaller home into a larger one. How long did it take to fill up this new larger home? I remember years ago when I moved into a larger home being elated to have extra space since I had been pretty crammed in my previous residence. Since I did not have furniture for my upstairs great room, it was delicious open space with room to dance and stretch uninhibited by furniture or walls that would restrict my movement.

One day there was a knock at the door and it turned out that a well-meaning friend had, unbeknownst to me, asked her husband to drop off a very pretty sofa she was now replacing. I knew it bothered her that I had a whole room upstairs with not one stick of furniture in it.

When the new couch arrived, I immediately acquiesced, giving up my physical roaming space that I loved so much. This action was so unconscious that I can only imagine some part of me also needed this space to be filled.

Apparently credit card companies also understand our need to fill space. Below is a partial advertisement from a marketing email I received not too long ago.

I have observed this same principle with clients and my younger self at different times where just having a credit card in the wallet can create an itch that needs to be scratched. All of a sudden, instead of paying for an item with actual money, it becomes easier to reach for the card as a way of deferring the impact of an impulsive purchase.

ACTION ITEM

If you have accumulated balances on your credit cards and you're making minimum payments, then refinancing your home mortgage to pay these in full can give you a fresh start. Without the credit card payments, you'll likely see a significant increase in your monthly cashflow and now have an opportunity to begin increasing your rainy day savings as we discussed in the previous chapter.

Another option to refinancing your debt is to begin paying down your credit card balances each month. I recommend paying down one at a time. Begin with the smallest debt you have and pay as much as you can until it's paid in full. Putting the bulk of your payments on one card will give you results that you can easily see and that will motivate you to continue. Once the smallest is paid in full, begin paying the next smallest and so on and so on. Sticking with this game plan takes commitment and strong determination and is not for the faint of heart. You will find yourself constantly tempted to abandon this debt reducing strategy. There may even be times when it feels too overwhelming to continue. However, with small steps and a strong commitment you can achieve independence from debt.

While paying off your credit cards is a smart move, closing them is not always a good idea. Ideally you want to continue to use one or two and then pay them off in full each month. This is because the credit scoring system will take the longevity of each account into consideration as well as your payment history when calculating your score. Plus, you will score higher having active credit.

Now that you've made the decision to pay off your credit cards you'll want to evaluate what is motivating your purchases - especially if you plan to pay for the goods or services with credit. Is there an emotional reason for the purchase or is this something you truly need? You might also consider walking away from the pending purchase and coming back on a different day if this item still matters to you. It's amazing how often the need for the item will dissipate when you take a step back.

Pitfall #4:

LATE PAYMENTS THAT RESULT FROM DISORGANIZATION OF FINANCIAL INFORMATION

"The Zen of organizing philosophy refers to
the creating of a calm, peace-filled,
and joyous environment."

–Regina Leeds

I can't tell you how many times I've reviewed a client's credit report and found recent late payments on one or more accounts that have caused a person's credit score to plummet. You may already know that the more recent the late payment the more drastic the impact on your score. This impact will however lessen over time.

For many of my clients, these late payments resulted from disorganization of their financial paperwork such as a bill that wasn't paid on time or the payment that was mailed to the wrong address. Setting up systems to prevent credit mishaps will inevitably save you money not only on your next mortgage but on other goods and services as well.

In addition to protecting your credit, having organized financial information at your fingertips will make your loan process easier when you plan to purchase a new home or refinance an existing mortgage.

Think you're organized?

- Do you open all of your mail or email when it arrives and sort out the important statements and letters from the rest of the clutter?
- If you are receiving billing statements via email, do you clear out your inbox on a regular basis? If not, it's easy to miss an important statement.
- Do you have a good system for paying your accounts when the email or paper statement arrives?
- Do you have easy access to all of your bank information including checking, savings and investment accounts?
- For each account, do you know the name of the institution, account number, account balance, and your current interest rate earned?

- Do you have easy access to all of your credit accounts including mortgages, credit cards, car payments, household utility bills, student loans, medical bills, and any person or institution to whom you owe money?
- Do you know the name of the institution/lender, account number, balance owed, interest rate and payment due dates for each credit account?

If you answered "YES" to the above questions, then you're most likely in good shape and unlikely to miss a payment because you forgot the due date.

Need help with organization? Then keep reading, because there are added benefits that can also free you from financial stress!

When your paperwork is organized, you know where you are financially, you know how much money you have available to spend, you know whether you can afford a particular purchase, and you know you are making informed financial decisions. Once you get organized you'll notice that you begin to weigh your buying decisions a little differently and with more objectivity. Before you know it, you'll find yourself in a place of calm and wisdom in your money matters.

Organization can be difficult when you are already feeling financially stressed. Maybe you are afraid to see how bad things really are. For instance, how much debt *do* you really owe?

Taking this important step will help you lay a solid foundation for future financial success because when you can see your money situation clearly, you can better strategize your next step. This next step could be the decision to refinance your home in order to consolidate your debt, to take out a business loan if you are experiencing a business slowdown, or to apply for a lower interest credit card so that you can transfer your high interest rate balances. When you see your true financial picture, both your conscious and your subconscious minds will help you find a solid approach towards improving your situation.

If you happen to own a small business, then organization of financial paperwork can be even more difficult. If you are like most small business owners, you wear many different hats throughout the day. You are most likely focused on making products, streamlining your services and taking care of your valuable clients. This is essential *time well spent*. However, for many entrepreneurs hiring a bookkeeper or investing in some type of accounting software to take care of the more mundane aspects of business is *money well spent*.

I once worked with a client whose kitchen table looked like his credit report. It was a mound of financial chaos with unopened bank statements and unopened bills. He was paying a much, much higher interest rate for his mortgage due to his poor credit. As a small business owner, he lacked the resources of a larger company and his time was spent with the day-to-day running of his business which left mail unopened and bills unpaid.

Hiring a bookkeeper to take care of mail, monthly billing and invoicing would have dramatically increased his cash flow and his credit score. Over time he would have eventually qualified for a much better interest rate, which would have lowered his mortgage payment considerably. In this particular case, the savings would have paid the bookkeeper's fee and then some.

Organizing tip:
Unopened mail or email will always appear more ominous than it really is. If you do not have a good system for mail, then begin a habit of opening your mail each time you collect it. Immediately toss out the junk and open everything else. If you are receiving your statements via email, it's often easier to pay the bill at the time the email is delivered. You could also create a bill folder and pop them in there. If you use this system you'll want some type of alert to make sure these bills aren't overlooked. Paying your bills will become easier once you have a system in place. I also bookmark all my accounts in a single folder in my browser; this makes it super easy to go through and check that nothing has been left unpaid.

Organizing tip:

These days you can elect to receive your statements via email or regular mail. Choose the method that allows you to best keep on top of this information and make sure that you are receiving all of your statements.

Organizing tip:

Have you ever tried to return an item to the store where it was purchased and not been able to find the receipt? Organizing all those receipts, bank deposit slips, bank statements, ATM receipts and paid billing statements is sometimes a job in itself. If you do not already have a system in place, then consider purchasing some large envelopes. Use one envelope for each month of the year. Label each envelope with the current month and then use it as a place for all those pieces of financial paper. You will be amazed at how easy it will be to find those important store receipts! You never know when you might need to access this information.

Organizing tip:

Consider using some financial software such as Quicken, QuickBooks or Microsoft Money to track expenses and balance your accounts. Using this type of system will easily allow you to categorize your expenses and keep an up-to-date record of all of your accounts—both bank accounts and credit accounts. You'll find it easier to reconcile your bank statement with this kind of software. When deciding on purchasing software, check with your bank to determine the most compatible version for their system.

If you decide to use one of these products, you will have an automatic accounting of where you are spending your money. Personally, I use software to track all my accounts, as it lets me see where I need to conserve and save. I make better choices because I have easy access to this information. For the self-employed folks who aren't ready to invest in bookkeeping services there are added benefits. You'll be able to easily access a profit & loss statement and balance sheet if you are applying for a home mortgage and you'll be prepared for your accountant come tax season.

ACTION ITEM

Do you know how much debt you owe? If not, make a list. Seeing this on paper can be so helpful, especially if you are strategizing your next financial planning step:

Creditor	Account Bal.	Monthly Payment	Int. Rate

1. Begin keeping a spending journal and start tracking how and when you're spending your money. This will tell you when and where you are most at risk for overspending. Separate out the necessary expenses from the more frivolous ones. Write down your mind set at the time of the purchase and notice whether there is a pattern emerging. For instance, my go-to if I'm feeling upset is always chocolate but this is only because I don't have the patience for shopping. Whereas for others, their go-to might be a large purchase that soothes an underlying emotion.

2. You could even continue this exploratory exercise by going through your credit card statements. Categorize each purchase noting purchase dates. This exercise will tell you how and when you are spending your money.

3. As you reflect on the above two exercises do you see a pattern emerging?

4. When do you think you are most at risk to overspend? *(For example, are you most likely to overspend when you've had an argument with your spouse, when you are feeling lonely or simply if you've had a bad day?)*

Pitfall #5:

COSIGNING FOR A FAMILY MEMBER OR FRIEND CAN NEGATIVELY IMPACT YOUR CREDIT

"The single most important ingredient in the recipe for success is transparency because transparency builds trust."

–Denis Morrison

Thinking about co-signing a loan for a family member or a friend who either can't get a loan on their own or wants to qualify for a lower interest rate? Did you know that co-signing for someone else can derail your own ability to obtain a reasonably priced mortgage?

It's true. Unfortunately, helping someone else in this way can cause you to pay more for your next mortgage. Worse, you might not even qualify.

Imagine this. You have done everything right to have an excellent credit history. You find a great property. You are ready to get the mortgage and you have everything lined up. Then you discover that the account you co-signed has been reported late on your credit report or is in default, and this account is now negatively impacting your credit scores. The damage has already been done because you co-signed for someone and they didn't tell you they weren't making their payments on time.

The person you are co-signing for is automatically considered the primary borrower for that loan. Lenders will require a co-signer when the primary borrower has insufficient credit history or insufficient income to qualify for the loan, or when their credit history shows late payments or credit problems. The most common types of loans that are co-signed are auto loans, real estate mortgages, and some credit cards. You may also be asked to co-sign for someone who is renting a home for the same reasons listed above. If they don't pay their rent and move out, you could potentially find an unexpected collection account on your report.

WHAT SEEMS HARMLESS MANY TIMES ISN'T!

This appears to be a harmless way to *help* someone who's in need. However, when it comes to money, what seems harmless many times isn't! When you co-sign a loan for someone this means that YOU (in addition to the primary borrower) are legally responsible for the repayment of the debt. No problem, right? You would expect to also be obligated? Once you sign the paperwork to co-sign a loan for someone, you're hopefully aware that if the primary borrower defaults on the loan then you are responsible for paying the balance. But you can't remedy a problem you don't know exists.

Considering that you're financially liable for the debt, you might expect that if a payment is late the lender would notify you as well as the primary borrower. Sadly, most lenders will not notify you regarding a late payment when you are the co-signer. They will only notify you when the loan is in default. This makes co-signing for someone else tricky since the billing statements and late notices are mailed only to the primary borrower.

DON'T MAKE ASSUMPTIONS!

> "Communicate with others as clearly as you can to avoid misunderstandings, sadness, and drama."

> *–Don Miguel Ruiz*

You would probably assume that the person you co-signed for would tell you if they couldn't make their payments on time. This might a reasonable assumption if they also fully understood the consequences to you of being late on the debt repayment.

Mostly I have found this not to be the case. The person you signed for is seldom fully aware of how their actions may impact your credit. It's also possible they feel too much shame or embarrassment to admit they aren't able to make their payments on time.

Unfortunately, you may not uncover the impact to your credit until *you* apply for a mortgage or other financing and discover your credit scores have tanked due to the co-signed loan being reported as late on your credit report!

HAVING PARAMETERS FOR YOUR GOOD DEED WILL PREVENT FUTURE REGRETS

Fully understanding the consequences can help you set up parameters for this good deed before it's too late. For instance, you may opt to pay the monthly bill yourself and have the borrower pay you directly each month. In this Internet age, you may even find it easier to obtain the account login information and monitor to make sure that the account is being paid on time.

Co-signing a loan can be a wonderful opportunity to help your daughter, your son or a relative establish credit. Staying mindful of the consequences of late payments and having notification agreements can prevent future regrets.

ACTION ITEM

If you have co-signed a loan for someone else:

1. Have a conversation with the person you co-signed for about the consequences to you if they are ever late. Often, they don't fully understand that if they are late on a payment, it will be reported on your credit report as well as theirs.

2. Monitor that the payments are being made on time.

3. Maintain open communication with the primary borrower. Be prepared to assist with payments without judgement.

Pitfall #6:

BUYING A HOME YOU CAN'T AFFORD

"Home is where love resides, and memories
are created, friends and family belong
and love never ends."

–author unknown

Shopping for a new home can be not only a life changing experience, but also a roller coaster ride for your emotions. You may have times of total excitement and hopefulness followed by frustration and disappointment. With all of these emotions in play, it's easy to allow a house to romance you into paying more than is comfortable for you and your family.

Consider this scenario. You've been disappointed by all the homes you've looked at and then you find a gem that's beckoning to become yours. Unfortunately, the cost is higher than you budgeted.

Putting this aside, you see yourselves moving into this wonderful gem. After all, it's in the right neighborhood and school district for your family and comes with amenities that could make your lives easier. There's more room for everyone than the other homes you've looked at and immediately you begin seeing possibilities for this additional space. You are simply in love!

Remember the old saying "When you're in love you're seeing the world through rose-colored glasses?" Falling madly in love with a home that is larger and more expensive than you had planned for can also mean that everything costs more. Unless you are in a position to invest a larger down payment, not only will your mortgage payment be higher than you originally anticipated, so will your utility bills, maintenance costs and possibly even your property taxes.

BE SURE TO INCLUDE YOUR LIFESTYLE IN YOUR HOME BUYING CALCULATIONS

Even though lender requirements to get a mortgage these days are tighter than they were a decade ago, you can still overcommit to a more expensive home and mortgage than you can reasonable afford. When qualifying you, the lender doesn't factor in your future plans. When deciding how much home to buy, take into consideration your lifestyle, the schools you want to send your children to or the college fund you are planning. These expenses are not part of any debt-to-income equation that is used to approve your mortgage financing.

You may decide you can justify the higher payment with the expectation of higher future income. This can be a risky expectation and something you don't want to bank on unless you have another strategy to draw from if things don't work out.

> "A good decision is based on knowledge and not on numbers."
>
> –Plato

When deciding on a new home, recognize that you don't want to end up having to borrow from your credit cards to make ends meet because you over-committed to a home.

If you have decided that the home is still the best option for your family then you'll want to come up with a plan to handle the additional expenses. You may even want to explore where you can cut costs to accommodate the higher payment and additional costs. Without another strategy for a larger and more expensive home, you could find yourself wallowing in high financial stress while trying to make your payments.

The impact of financial stress can be profound, not only guaranteeing sleepless nights but also limiting your creativity while impacting your health and relationships if it continues long term. Of course, you could consider a more affordable home with potential to grow in step with your family and income instead.

ACTION ITEM

Do some homework before you buy:

1. When buying a home, take the time before you begin shopping and honestly look at your current expenses and anticipate how those might change after you've purchased the new home. Consider what new expenses might be involved and if there are others that could become obsolete with the new home purchase.

2. Once you have a home in mind, contact the local utility companies and ask them about the average cost for heating and cooling the home. This will give you an idea of how much you might be paying for utilities for that particular home.

3. Property taxes vary between properties, so be sure to ask your realtor how much the taxes are for each home you are considering. A lender should also be able to give you this information. Otherwise, you can get it from the county.

4. Invest in a home inspection. This is money well worth the cost even if the home is new construction. The home inspection will not only show you what needs to be repaired, but you'll get a reliable idea of future maintenance costs.

5. Check with your accountant about whether or not you might qualify for a home mortgage interest deduction and how that might impact your tax bill. For example, if you are a salaried employee, you may be able to choose how much money you want your employer to withhold from your paycheck. The higher the number of allowances, the less money is withheld, which means a larger paycheck. This additional money could accommodate a higher payment if you are stretching to buy the bigger and more expensive home. However, a word of caution here. If you increase your allowances, there is always the possibility you could end up owing taxes at the end of the year. If you claim fewer allowances, you may receive a very nice refund that can be put towards a new roof, if needed, or a college fund.

6. Talk with a lender before you begin house hunting to find out how much home you might qualify for. They will also be able to give you an idea of your anticipated monthly housing costs.

Pitfall #7:

SIGNING UP FOR AN ACCELERATED PAYMENT PLAN WITH A MORTGAGE SERVICE COMPANY

"There is nothing like staying at home
for real comfort."

–Jane Austen

For most people, a monthly mortgage payment is a way of life. Others dream of owning their home outright. If you are one of these people, you may be considering steps to ensure that your mortgage is paid off early.

This is where you might be tempted to sign up with a mortgage service company for an accelerated payment plan. However, think twice before you sign on the dotted line! You can end up unnecessarily paying more than you bargained for.

HOW IT WORKS

Setting up an accelerated plan through a mortgage service company is expensive as they charge fees you might not have penciled into your initial calculations. For instance, you'll pay a setup fee of $399 or more, then there will be a small fee for debiting your account for each withdrawal, a verification fee to verify your account number and there may even be late payment fees if you are tardy with a payment.

These companies don't have any magic formulas for getting you out of debt. When you're on the plan, you'll pay half your mortgage payment every two weeks—that equals 26 half payments per year. If you do the math you'll see that 26 half payments per year means you'll end up paying one extra payment that goes towards your principle. This will pay off your 30-year mortgage in approximately 22 years.

While this sounds like a wonderful idea, paying off your mortgage early is not for everyone. First, you will need to have the additional cashflow to accommodate that extra annual payment that occurs when on the plan. Also, if you have ongoing credit card debt, it makes better sense to accelerate these payments before you begin whittling down your mortgage.

You may discover that the extra cash you're using to pay off your mortgage could get a better return if invested in another way. This is a great conversation to have with your financial planner and your accountant. They may have some better options available for you.

If, after a little research, you've decided that paying off your mortgage early is in your best interest, then why not do it yourself and save some money?

You can easily achieve the same result without the additional costs by simply setting up the plan yourself. Or to lessen the need for discipline, why not set up an auto-pay on your bank's bill pay. Either way the reward will make this worthwhile.

Remember you only need to make one extra payment per year to reduce the length of your mortgage. Here are three ways to accomplish this. Pick one and you'll build additional equity in no time.

1. Make an extra payment with your tax refund, work bonus or dip into your savings for the additional payment.

2. Increase each payment by 1/12th and by the end of a year you will have accomplished the same as one extra payment.

3. Pay half your amortized payment every two weeks. There will be a couple of months in the year where you end up paying 1.5 payments.

There are some additional benefits to accelerating your mortgage payments and building equity faster even if you don't keep the mortgage full term. If you sell the home, you'll walk away with more cash and if you refinance the home the additional payments you have made could potentially drop your loan to value, which could in turn give you a better interest rate or allow more cash out if an emergency arises.

ACTION ITEM

If the idea of paying off your mortgage early sounds viable to you then here are a few homework items you'll want to consider before you begin:

1. Grab a pencil and paper and prepare a budget for yourself. Do you have the additional cash flow to accommodate the extra payment each year?

2. Meet with a financial planner and your accountant to discuss what other options might be available to you. Also discuss the pros and cons of accelerating your mortgage payments for your particular situation.

3. Check with your lender before beginning to ensure the extra payment is applied to the principle and ask if they would charge you an additional fee if you were to make biweekly payments.

Be Prepared!

"The future belongs to those who prepare for it."

–Ralph Waldo Emerson

I once read a quote that said, "Prepare and prevent, don't repair and repent." The author is unknown but whoever said this might have had some insight into what's needed when applying for a mortgage. Being prepared before you begin your loan application will make the loan approval and funding process much easier.

When you apply for a conventional mortgage, the lender will review your income, assets and liabilities. They will also verify your identity. Before you begin the process make sure that addresses and names are correct on all your financial information. Sometimes these documents don't get updated when you move because so often our statements are delivered to us via the computer. These documents include your homeowner's insurance statement, bank statements, retirement accounts and any other financial information.

Make sure your proof of identity documents are showing your correct name and address. These documents would include your driver's license or any other government-issued ID that you plan to use as proof of identity.

Repair and repent is exactly what happens when incorrect information is submitted to an underwriter. More conditions will be triggered before they will fully approve your loan. The more conditions they require, the more arduous the process and the longer the loan will take to fund. An example of this might be if you are refinancing a mortgage on the home that you are now living in, but your driver's license and bank statements show a different address. You may be asked to write a letter of explanation and provide proof that the home you are financing is indeed owner-occupied.

TIPS TO MAKE THE APPLICATION PROCESS EASY

When you are gathering your documentation, you will want to include all pages of the document you are submitting. For instance, the lender will want all pages of your bank statements, including any blank pages, not just the summary page.

If the bank statements show any large deposits that are not income related, the lender will want to verify the source of these. If you sold something and deposited a check or cash, the lender may require a copy of the check, bill of sale, company invoice or advertisement copy plus a written explanation. The origins of cash deposit can be tricky to prove and can cause delays or even prevent the funding of your loan if you aren't able to provide a paper trail for these deposits.

An example of this might be, you sell a car and use the proceeds towards your down-payment for the purchase of a home. You then deposit these funds into your bank account. In this case, as well as similar circumstances, you'll want to be prepared to produce a paper trail to explain the deposit.

"The ache for home lives in all of us, the safe place where we can go as we are and not be questioned."

–Maya Angelou

COMMON DOCUMENTS REQUIRED

Here is a list of common documents that might be needed once you have made a loan application. This is a general list of what might be required to submit your loan to an underwriter. Please disregard whatever documentation doesn't apply to your situation. For instance, if you are a salaried employee then you won't have a business tax return, profit & loss statement or balance sheet.

Income

- Most recent two years' personal federal tax returns (1040s) complete with all pages
- Most recent two years' business tax returns all schedules—all worksheets (only if self-employed)
- Year to date profit & loss statement and balance sheet for current year (only if self-employed)
- Last two years' W2s and 1099s
- Most recent paystubs covering a full month of employment
- Advisor letter if income is coming from an annuity
- Copy of most recent disability award letter
- Social Security award letter if using this income to qualify
- Proof of alimony filed in court if using this income to qualify

Assets

- Most recent two months' bank statements for each account (all pages)
- A recent statement for any retirement, investment or money market accounts

Misc.
- Current mortgage statements for each mortgage
- Property tax statement for each home you own
- Copy of your homeowner's insurance declaration page for both flood and home insurance for each home you own
- Two forms of government-issued ID, such as a copy of your driver's license and social security card or passport
- Copy of lease agreement if renting
- Documentation for source of funds for your down payment. As discussed, the lender will want to know where this money is coming from and whether it's documented. For instance, are you withdrawing money from your savings or checking account to use towards your down payment or is this down payment coming from the sale of an asset, a gift or an inheritance?Prior To Applying for a Mortgage

> "Before anything else,
> preparation is the key to success."
>
> *–Alexander Graham Bell*

If you are planning on applying for a mortgage within the next six months, it's also a good idea to slow down your borrowing. The more debts you have, the less home you'll qualify for. I recommend that you don't apply for any new credit as that can sometimes impact your ability to qualify for the mortgage.

Don't wait until the last minute to organize your paperwork as this will delay the underwriting process and will also prevent you from being issued a timely loan approval. With a competitive housing market, many sellers want to know that you are qualified to buy their home. Having a prequalification or a preapproval letter with your offer to purchase makes you a much more competitive buyer.

Once you have made your loan application and started the loan process, don't change anything that is relevant to your financial situation unless you talk to your loan officer first. For instance, don't buy a new car, apply for new credit or change jobs if at all possible. Don't make the mistake of assuming that once your loan is approved you can buy an item that results in a debt increase before the loan actually funds and records. The lender will refresh your credit report before they fund your mortgage.

If you do find yourself in a situation where you need to make a change, either a new debt or a new job, discuss the circumstances with your loan officer immediately to prevent closing delays.

Before You Shop for A New Home

"Home is the nicest word there is"

–Laura Ingalls Wilder

Shopping for a new home can be exciting since there are many reasons why you might be planning a move. For instance, you decide to own your own home rather than continuing to rent. Perhaps you are selling your home and moving to a new town or neighborhood. Or you may be looking to accommodate your growing family. Whatever your reason for buying a new home, once you find that special gem, you'll want to make sure the odds are in your favor of having your offer accepted. This becomes even more important when there are other offers also coming to the seller's table.

YOUR FIRST STEP

It's a good idea before you begin house hunting to speak with a lender and to get prequalified. You can do this either by contacting a mortgage broker or by going directly to your bank. I discuss the differences in the next chapter.

Getting pre-qualified means discussing your overall financial picture with a lender. They will ask you questions about your income and assets, and review your credit. They will also ensure that your debt-to-income ratios meet the acceptable limits. These debt-to-income ratios indicate to the lender whether or not you have enough income to cover your monthly mortgage payments as well as other monthly debt obligations for the price range you have in mind.

Debt to income ratios are calculated by adding your anticipated new home payment and all your other monthly and recurring credit obligations, then dividing this number by your gross monthly income. Your anticipated new home payment includes not only the projected monthly principle and interest payment as well as your monthly property tax amount, homeowner's insurance, mortgage insurance and (or) homeowner's dues if applicable.

During this pre-qualification process, you will have an opportunity to discuss not only your price range but also the payment that you will be most comfortable with in regards to your lifestyle and other financial obligations. If you recall, in Chapter 6 we discussed the importance of having a house payment that also works for your budget. At this time the lender will discuss with you the loan programs that might be available to you depending on how much money you have to invest as a down payment while also factoring in your mortgage goals and lifestyle. From here you can start house hunting and are ready to make an offer on a home.

IN TODAY'S SOPHISTICATED HOUSING MARKET

In today's sophisticated housing market many sellers are more comfortable accepting an offer from a potential buyer who has been pre-qualified by the lender (including a prior review of the buyer's income and asset documentation). This is sometimes referred to as a pre-approval since documentation has been reviewed in advance.

Taking his extra step upfront can sometimes be the deciding factor in having your offer accepted. Providing this information to the lender at the beginning of the process will not only give the lender a more accurate overview of your financial picture, but they can also advise you in advance of any additional documentation that might be needed to ensure a smooth loan approval and funding process.

Getting pre-qualified or pre-approved in advance is beneficial since once you have provided your income, asset and credit information to the lender, they will be able to provide you with a pre-qualification/pre-approval letter. Having this type of letter in hand makes your realtor's job so much easier at the negotiation table.

ROCK SOLID OFFER

What if you wanted to offer the seller even more of a guarantee that you are the most qualified buyer for their house? You can take an extra step by asking your lender to submit your application with all of your income, asset and credit documentation to an underwriter for a loan approval even though you don't yet have a property selected. While not all lenders are able to offer this option, many do. Ask your lender or mortgage broker about this.

While I can never predict what a seller may do, having a loan approval before you make an offer shows the seller that you are a rock-solid buyer and that may increase your chances of getting accepted into contract.

The Difference Between a Mortgage Broker and a Bank?

Now that you are ready to go talk with a lender about getting pre-qualified for your next home, you may be wondering where to start. You can go directly to your bank and make an application or you can opt to work with a mortgage broker instead. The main difference between a broker and a bank is that a mortgage broker works with many different banks. In other words, a mortgage broker may have more options available for you than your bank when it comes to securing the best mortgage for your situation.

Not all banks underwrite mortgages in the same way. This is because in addition to the program guidelines for the particular loan you have applied for, they superimpose their own standards of what's acceptable to them.

ABC Bank may have a minimum credit score requirement of more than 620 for a certain type of loan even when the actual program guidelines only require a credit score of 580. You may wander into another bank that will fund loans with a slightly lower credit score but are stricter on their debt-to-income ratio requirements. As such, each bank has their own criteria based on their comfort zone and the types of loans they like or don't like.

Mortgage rates and terms can vary slightly between banks, but when it comes down to who is most likely to fund your mortgage, a mortgage broker often has the advantage. Typically, they will look for the lender who is the best fit for your particular scenario. If that lender happens to deny your mortgage loan request due to something that gets uncovered during underwriting, without missing a beat a broker may quickly resubmit your loan to a more sympathetic lender.

In addition, because of their larger and more diverse network, a broker can sometimes get loans funded that have been denied by a bank. This ability to move quickly from one lender to the next results in timelier "fundings" along with competitive rates and terms.

About the Author

"You would make a really great mortgage broker," my friend Kathy Silva told me in 1991. I was shocked. Up until this point I had programmed computers, taught computer skills and other related classes, provided software & computer education, written training manuals and sold real estate, but finance had never been on my radar.

That seed grew into a career path that so far has spanned more than two decades. Within a year I opened my own mortgage firm, helping homeowners get the financing they needed to either purchase a home or to refinance an existing loan.

Looking back, I now realize how my previous background (which relied on logic as well as thinking outside the box) prepared me for the world of finance. Having experience as an instructor in my earlier years also taught me the value of helping clients to understand the process (as well as their own relationship with money) in order to become more attractive to lenders.

Contact
Tracia Larimer
Azara Capital Solutions, LLC
Email: tracia@azaracapitalsolutions.com
Web: www.AzaraCapitalSolutions.com
(541) 241-8344

Legal
Azara Capital Solutions, LLC NMLS# 1577943
Tracia Larimer
Mortgage Broker
NMLS# 1507306

EQUAL HOUSING
LENDER